A STARVED HEART

A STARVED HEART

GENEVIEVE LARDIZABAL

A PUBLICATION OF THE POETRY BOX®

Editing & Book Design: Shawn Aveningo Sanders
Cover Design: Shawn Aveningo Sanders
Cover Image: Veliza Ivanof (via Unsplash)
Fear Image: Kasper Rasmussen (via Unsplash)
Anger Image: Camila Quintero (via Unsplash)
Depression Image: Yuris Alhumaydy (via Unsplash)
Redemption Image: Aida L. (via Unsplash)
Author Photo: Stacey Jenkins

ISBN: 978-1-956285-30-7
Library of Congress Control Number: 2022923869
Printed in the United States of America.
Wholesale Distribution by Ingram Group

Published by The Poetry Box®, March 2023
Portland, Oregon
https://thepoetrybox.com

*To my parents who were there for me
even when I didn't want them to be.*

*To my brother for loving me
even when I was difficult to love.*

*To Natalie, Dr. Bermudez, Ginger, Dr. Kessel, Heather,
and all the staff at the Eating Recovery Center
(in Bellevue and Denver)
for helping me find myself again.*

CONTENTS

Introduction 11
Songs to Accompany the Poems 13

FEAR

2017-2018 19
What Made My Eating Disorder So
  Desirable 21
Six Days of Starving 24
Talking to My Eating Disorder 26
Seattle Children's Hospital 27
In My Mothers Voice 30
Seventh Grade 31
Cages 33
My Mind as a House 36
My Abusive Eating Disorder 37
OCD 38

ANGER

Nobody Believing I Had an Eating
  Disorder 43
Panic Attacks in the Hospital 45
Denver Children's Hospital 46
To My First Boyfriend 48
Mirrors at Different Times in My Life 49

DEPRESSION

Virtual Visits in Treatment 53
To My Childhood Best Friend 54

The Reality behind Instagram Posts   56

To My Friend I Met in Treatment   59

In the Voice of My Brother   61

Silence Is Louder Than Shrieks   62

Eating Disorder   63

February 10th, 2020: In My Brother's
    Voice   65

Insomnia in Treatment   67

Treatment Cycle   68

Growing Up   70

The Cold of Anorexia   72

Suicide Note   73

Treatment in Colorado   74

Taking Up Space   76

"God Has a Plan"   78

Dear Depression   79

On the Way to Denver Eating Recovery
    Center   80

Room-Based Care   81

REDEMPTION

Genevieve as a Ghost Watching Her
    Eating Disorder   85

To Dad   87

Gratitude   88

A Letter to a Song   89

Happiness   90

Going Home from Treatment in Denver   91

March through the Years   92

Spring Heart   96

Things I Was Once Afraid of   98

I Deserve(d) Better   100

Dream   101

To My Twelve-Year-Old Self   102

Perspective   104
Toxic Love   105
Stories Are Meant to Be Heard   106
I Choose   107

❧

Early Praise for *A Starved Heart*   111
About the Author   113
About The Poetry Box˚   115

INTRODUCTION

I HAVE FALLEN DOWN THE PIT of desolation countless times in my life—times in my life when I believed I had hit the bottom. I was twelve when I was diagnosed with Anorexia Nervosa. The diagnosis felt ominous. At such a young age, I was consumed by the fear that my life might end. Through the years, my pain continued to pull me further into disorder.

I never thought I'd recover. I pushed against the idea for years because I believed wholeheartedly it was unattainable. I had this idea stuck in my brain that choosing recovery would be a movie moment. All the lights would dim, except for the spotlight on me; soft music would start playing; and I would finally realize what I'm doing is unsustainable. It was a difficult idea for me to grasp that it was never meant to be like that. It took digging inside the depths of my mind to find a voice that wasn't tainted by disorder and make decisions for my future that would push me in the direction of recovery.

This book is my hand reaching out to show others they are not alone in their struggle. As one follows through my journey, they can see the light start to peer out, and the love start to commence, after much hardship. I also firmly believe eating disorders are the most misunderstood disorder, and I want to break the stigma, and provide education on how eating disorders affect one's life.

It is vital to understand this journey carries difficult ideas to swallow and potential triggers for things like restriction, treatment, purging, self-harm, and suicidal ideation. I try not to go into heavy detail, and in no way would I ever want to glamorize these tough situations. It is important to read cautiously. Protecting oneself should always be the priority.

As one reads further into my journey, they will notice a consistent use of the pronoun "him." This represents the Eating Disorder voice in my head. At the start of my sickness the disorder and I were intertwined, his thoughts were mine, and my voice was his. But as the years went on, there was a separation from his voice and mine; I heard a loud, booming male voice in my head telling me how to destroy myself. I

[. . .]

thought of it as an abusive boyfriend, constantly putting me down, and making me use behaviors damaging to my body and mind. I had a misconception that after I chose recovery, the voice would dissipate. It has been two years that I've actively been in recovery, and I still hear that voice sometimes. The goal shouldn't be to never hear it again because I made that mistake and would freeze with fear when it came back. One's goal should be to know how to talk back to the disorder and understand that these are just thoughts—one can choose whether to buy into them or not.

I found I had one prominent emotion for each stay in treatment. The first year, I was terrified. Every screaming fight I got into with my parents, every tear, every panic attack had the underlying emotion of fear. The second year I was enraged. I felt like everyone was against me. I'd always been determined, and I was so dead set on killing every ounce of love in me and becoming my disorder, that I looked at support as a roadblock.

By the third year, I fell into a deep depression, and in a way, sadness opened a path to success. Because when I was afraid, I held onto my disorder like it was a security blanket. When I was angry, I never let anyone help me. I had such hatred for recovery and didn't have any hope left. Through the depression and pain, I finally realized how much my eating disorder was destroying me. I had reached such a state of vulnerability that every word I said, every thought I had, every action I made was controlled by my eating disorder. It caused me such pain that I started to realize the reason for my eating disorder in the first place was my attempt to find happiness, acceptance, control, and safety. My disorder gave me none of those.

Songs to Accompany the Poems

Music has been impactful on my journey. Ever since I was 10 years old, I've had music playing. If you like to listen to music while reading, here are some suggestions for songs I feel fit each poem.

Fear

"The Great Gig in the Sky" by Pink Floyd
"Beginner's Luck" by Maribou State
"Spurs Edit" by AL" by 90
"Valasy" by Nünberg
"Strawberry" by Doss
"Drawn to the Blood" by Sufjan Stevens
"Resonance" by Home
"Smthng" by Muddy Monk
"For the Damaged Coda" (Extra Track) by Blonde Redhead
"Darling" by tomppabeats
"Penelope" by Pinback

Anger

"House of the Risin' Sun" by Bob Dylan
"Garfield" by sunflwr
"Channel 1 Suite" by The Cinematic Orchestra
"Jewel" by Cranes
"Anemone" by The Brian Jonestown Massacre

[. . .]

Depression

"Undress" by Passing Currents
"Ylang Ylang" by FKJ & (((O)))
"John My Beloved" by Sufjan Stevens
"In My Head" by Bedroom
"Rosyln" by Bon Iver & St. Vincent
"Scientist Studies" by Death Cab for Cutie
"Title Track" by Death Cab for Cutie
"Nutshell" by Alice in Chains
"Between the Bars" by Elliot Smith
"Je Te Laisserai des Mots" by Patrick Watson
"Waiting for Cars" by Soccer Mommy
"Time Is the Enemy" by Quantic
"Private Presley" by Peach Pit
"All of Me Wants All of You" by Sufjan Stevens
"The Wisp Sings" by Winter Aid
"Shadow" by Wild Nothing
"Grown" by Soccer Mommy
"Count to Five" by Bedroom
"Ram On" by Paul & Linda McCartney

REDEMPTION

"As We Bloom" by Strawberry Guy
"It Never Entered My Mind" by Miles Davis
"Portofino" by Raymond Scott
"Babe" by Evenings
"Death of the Phone Call" by Whatever, Dad
"beatdepression" pt.1" by sunflwr
"Scarborough Fair / Canticle" by Simon & Garfunkel
"Evergreen" by Richy Mitch & The Coal Miners
"Welcome and Goodbye" by Dream, Ivory
"Silver Soul" by Beach House
"*Les Filles Désir*" by Vendredi sur Mer
"Sweet Disposition" by The Temper Trap
"Trembling Hands" by The Temper Trap
"History's Door" by Husky
"How It Ends" by DeVotchKa

FEAR

2017-2018

Why was it that when boys made fat jokes they roamed in packs?
And their words didn't roll off their tongues,
but instead rose into howls.

It was May when I heard it for the first time,
vicious snarls of the word fat.
Rolling out lists
Kathrine, Anna, Beth
her stomach looks like a balloon,
how can she walk?

The mirror glowered at me,
morphing into more than just a reflection,
even the size of my pinky finger started to gnaw at me.
The list of girls they spit out must have had my name on the top
in big bold letters.

In June,
my mind was being strangled by tape measures
and drowned in Diet Coke.
Endless laps,
whistles still wrang in my ears even miles from the pool.

I ran even when my legs started to wobble in the hot sun
and my lungs begged for rest.
I told myself it was worth it.
I would stop when I got there.
But the chase of skinny never ends when you don't know what
you truly look like.

I asked my mom under the August sun
Why can I see numbers floating up the straw every time I take a sip?
She brushed it off,
because how can you admit to yourself your baby is sick?

[. . .]

October struck heavy on my weakening figure,
it was Halloween,
my friends sat in the kitchen,
carrots and hummus spilling out of their mouths.

I sat in my hollow room,
tears spilling down my funeral dress.
I can't eat Mom.
She promised to get me help
but at this point I was submerged.

November began with my name hanging under
Anorexia Nervosa
The doctors told me I could no longer swim,
you will faint
and I scoffed in their faces,
I am fine.

two days later
whistles went in and out of my hearing
as I sunk to the bottom,
all I could hear were faint yells swirling around my limp body.
it is now January 23rd
13 days after my 13th birthday
my legs crossed on the hospital bed.

Vigorously,
thoughts swirl in my weak mind,
but one question keeps shouting at me,
gluing itself to the back of my eyes
and forcing its way into the thick of my brain,
over and over, it asks,
Why did you give those boys so much power?

WHAT MADE MY EATING DISORDER SO DESIRABLE

1. ACCEPTANCE

My middle school had vines hanging from the ceiling.
The wolves would sit and howl on the balcony overlooking the
    lunchroom
and shake the school with their obnoxious laughter.

And the lions would groom themselves ten times over and whisper
    about the leopard across the room.

I couldn't comprehend the different shades of our fur,
how badly I pleaded for my body to go from orange to gold
and glisten beneath the sunlight
rather than make my stripes more visible

They never hung out with people that looked like me.
It was always the ones who could be their reflection in the river
    staring back at them that caught their attention.

Every drop of spirit I had left was swallowed by the shower drain
my soul that had once flashed electric blue
had turned to a sterile white

I was no longer a tiger,
but neither was I a lion

[. . .]

2. Control

My imagination leaked out of the cracks of my skull into a silver
    bucket.
Every birthday I would hear drips pound against the bottom of the
    bucket like a ticking clock.

When I was young,
birthday candles were more than just wax,
fairies lived in the forest by my house.
and mermaids swam deep in the underwater city.

It was when I was 11 that I felt the shell of childhood crack off my
    back.

Crimson tides ran down my legs,
blades of black prickly grass now showed up all over my body,
even on my upper lip.

I had no grasp on the reins of my changing body.
I needed something I could mold like play dough,
something gratifying,
something beautiful

I looked to my left
old paintings, schoolwork, and journals were stacked in a neat pile,
My mind was in a flurry of possibilities,
an artist, a professor, a poet.
but something called out to me on my right,
it wasn't the gold frame around it that filled the gap in my soul,
or the way it hung so delicately on the wall
it was how I immediately knew the girl staring back at me would be
    my favorite project.
Choosing beauty over passion was my biggest mistake.

3. SAFETY

The world still has its case and plastic packaging as a child,
whether asking my mom on a walk home from school why the leaves
   have turned yellow, or why we never see her mom and dad.

When I heard the word cancer
I felt I was being sucked into a black hole of fate.
That I would relive her childhood
and the walls of my empty home would suffocate me,
my mom's loud belly laugh would be nothing but a mere memory
and my dad's jokes would lift up the chimney to the clouds
alone for eternity.

I was 12 when I felt the most alone,
kids swarming the halls,
pushing past each other while screaming to their temporary best
   friend.
Even with the chaos,
all the voices were muffled

no matter how many of them slipped into my ears
and how many words left my mouth,
I knew I was on my own.

He visited me one night.
His paper white skin dripped into mine
I could feel my soul being sucked out from his vacuum teeth,
when he spoke, he said,
You don't have to be alone anymore. I will stick with you forever.
I should have said no.

Six Days of Starving

The morning call is harsher than I remembered.
The mist cutting through my sleep
and dragging in through my covered window.
Get up
I hear the nurse say this sharply,
blades of grass I can no longer lie in.

But when I stand
my head bounces onto the cement floor
crevasses of light dragging my vision in.

And I curl on the floor,
my knees to my face,
my spine hitting against the wall
each vertebrae trying to rip through my thin skin.

It's been six days without food or water,
I miss the feeling of my taste buds tingling,
and my stomach's rocky waves coming to a halt.

At eight am I drank a sip of water.
and for five minutes I could breathe without my heart aching,
I could stand up without falling,

but by minute three
I wondered what a deep ache would feel like
one where my insides go through the paper shredder of starvation
and all I can hear is my pulse slowly dropping.

I sat with my back to the orange painted walls,
closing my weary eyes
and for a moment my mind walked into a clearing.
I could hear the wind,
It groaned softly,
I could barely make out the words it sang,
and then I heard it.
There is nothing beautiful about dying.

TALKING TO MY EATING DISORDER

Somehow the stillness of the morning shakes me.
It's as if silence is louder than shrieks.

You grasp my back,
Bunching my shirt into a handful
and I feel full even on an empty stomach.

I take a whiff of your breath.
It smells like gunpowder,
at least we have that in common.

Seattle Children's Hospital

1. Waiting Room

The walls were cold,
kids with bright blue masks and glares.
A lot of tears
and crying babies.

I held onto my dad's coat while I scanned the floor for my mom.
My breath kept running out of my lungs
and getting stuck under my shoes,
tripping over my own panic.
I looked at the opening doors,
widening their big jaws and exhaling the February air.
Though I don't remember them ever inhaling it.

I saw a mother stroke the back of her daughter's hair,
and whisper over the droning TV that nobody was watching.
She had curly hair that framed the face of pain.

And my trance was snapped by the monotone voice,
they're ready for you, Genevieve.

[. . .]

2. EMERGENCY ROOM

Everything was duller than the pictures
I whipped out my phone immediately in the car ride before,
trying to let the room settle in my veins so I wouldn't be so shocked.

They showed bright orange rooms,
nurses with their arms resting on counters
laughing while sipping coffee.

When I arrived
there were strands of lights that made it impossible to tell
whether it was morning or night.
Windowless rooms,
and nurses running in and out of doors.
I searched for smiles
but their tired eyes hung like spiders
and their mouths moved like roars with no sound.

I saw kids being rolled by,
screaming,
blue straps tying them down
and mesh bags over their hands and head.
I looked at my mom.
She was still holding her gray coat and yellow bag
and my mouth was open,
trying to breathe out what I just saw
but instead my voice broke as I whispered,
what have I done Mom? I want to go home.

3. PSYCH WARD

Milk white gloves gripped onto my skin.
No person in them
just dead eyed nurses telling me to stay still.

My stomach rolled,
my heart pulsing in my jaw.
The pain ran through my nose
up to the top of my head.

Little boys threatened my life with plastic knives.
I watched as they threw chairs,
bent over backwards
biting their teeth sharp.

Tears floated down my throat,
a small spore of existence
flattened by the flickering lights of the hospital.

I cried into peppered chairs,
my body bent,
thinning hair covering my hollow cheeks.

My mother would visit me,
Where did I go wrong?
But I would just stare at her with lightless eyes,
cowering in my own rancid head,
gnawing on my gums
I beg for freedom,
her eyes well up with tears,
she places her forehead against mine and says softly,
it's in your hands but your fists stay clenched.

In My Mother's Voice

I really thought I could save you.
Even when your eyes turned black
and your once tan skin had faded to paper white,
even when I saw you pull out clumps of hair
and your legs turned purple.

I truly believed I'd be able to save you.

I tried everything.
Writing letters every day,
not knowing that every heartfelt word I wrote
would not be able to reach you
because your brain was lacking the fuel to work.

I would visit you often
bringing my funnel and trying to cram memories
of how you used to be through your ears.
But it was like you couldn't hear at all.

3 hours I would sit at the kitchen island
and watch your mouth tear into two.
Screams and shrieks exhaling your lips.

I miss Genevieve.
The girl that would slip apology letters under my door
when she got in trouble,
and had the ability to talk to strangers like they were lifelong friends.
Her loud boisterous laugh now floats as a memory
when I would do anything to hear it again.
She was my yellow balloon in a sea of gray,
my Picasso in a world of Da Vinci's,
but most of all my daughter.

SEVENTH GRADE

I remember looking at the school holding my breath,
I was so obsessed with killing the chubby me with blunt bangs
that I didn't want people to recognize me.

My hair was in two braids that swished on my back.
I wore a top that showed off my stomach,
and pants that hugged my thighs.

But I still had energy.
I smiled in class,
laughed at Mr. Dorson and his comical sweatshirts.

I even sat next to a boy with honey brown eyes,
and whispered with him during the meditations in homeroom.

It is December now,
this black science table feels cold against my palms.
The clock with red numbers watches above me as I count my pulse.
My fingers pressing into the skin on my neck.
I have 40 written on my notebook seven times,
because it just can't be true.

The girls next to me asked me what I had for breakfast,
and I looked at them wondering if they could hear my stomach
rumbling and feel the dizziness that passes through me
everytime I lift my head.

Instead I just left without answering
and walked by the girl in the glass trophy case
that is supposed to be my reflection.

I stopped talking to the boy with honey brown eyes,
I couldn't lift my head enough to speak.

[. . .]

Kids chanted the depressed girl when I'd walk into class,
they laughed and watched my eyes spill over with tears.
I tried to remember having a sense of humor,
but I couldn't imagine how much energy it would take to do that.

I thought being thin would make me happy,
but even smiling makes me feel like I'm lying.

CAGES

1. AT THE ZOO

We walked in unison
through tunnels.
Black, red, and blue cars shattering the delicate silence.

As we reached the zoo,
my cousin leapt
pressing her head on glass cages
beckoning the monkey to respond to her,
entertain her.

But boredom called for her to leave
and my soul burned in my pocket,
a wide hole in my thin pants.

I pressed my hand softly against the glass
and closed my eyes.

When my lids lifted, I saw him staring at me,
orange tufts of hair on his head,
weary eyes begging to close, giving up on freedom.

[. . .]

2. At the Antique Store

My mind had space to think with the quiet footsteps across the floor.
Old teacups with detailing,
recliner chairs that welcomed you when you sat down with a bounce
    of tricks.

Porcelain dolls in small corners,
eyes that followed me around the room.

I stood in front of tall glass cases my eyes tracing the lock.
I felt a body warm up beside me,
why can't we touch them?
I asked, staring at the emeralds.
to protect them.
I stood,
watching the green reflect jumping fish on the wall,
reciting the words in my head,
Protection.

3. Trying to Escape Treatment Centers

I pined for fresh air to cascade through each limb,
to feel grass in between my toes
and look at the buildings tower over me
and realize just how tiny humans are.

I haven't been outside in 5 months.
I didn't understand why they wanted to protect me from it
I didn't need protection
I need more than beige colored walls and frosted over windows.

I felt my soul jumping against my rib cage, needing so badly
for somewhere to breathe.

My weary eyes no longer begged to close
but do what the orangutan should have done
bang against the glass and beg for freedom.

I got ready to leave,
slipping my black puffer jacket on
and sliding into my white sneakers.

I imagined running out of treatment center doors,
but my mind got caught on the coat hook of no matter how far I run,
my eating disorder will follow.

He is the one keeping me caged,
not the hospital.

MY MIND AS A HOUSE

My fingers traced over the cracked tiles,
and stroked the leaky faucet from where you screamed,
forcing words down my throat,
tugging at the wires from the ceiling.

The house so stained with your hatred all the walls are bright
    vermilion.
You tied my arms into knots,
my spine pressed up against the bare sewing machine,
stitching my limbs together with empty words of *I love you*.

Light waves through the room,
where you lay in between cotton sheets,
while the TV static hums in tune with your breathing

I fall into a heap of sighs on the floor,
my head against the kitchen counter,
the absence of noise nesting like a promise,
I will never yell again.

MY ABUSIVE EATING DISORDER

The air does not stir,
red smeared across the sky
bending down to whisper *it's not safe*,
but I waved my hand in dismay,
collecting my eyes in the palms of my hands.

No need for sight when I can smell the wine bottles rolling on the
    floor,
and taste the nickels tumbling under my tongue
I already began to sense the night growing heavier.

I thought back to the beginning,
where we swam in clear pools,
my feet kicked back,
diving headfirst into his arms.
Promises licked me and my shrinking body.
Now I sit,
his grip growing firmer on my shoulder.

I look around our tumbling house,
the shattered plates,
Stained with my meek shadows
the name
crybaby,
still lingering in the air.

His breath like the kiss of rotten pears,
I burrow in the nape of his neck,
my lungs shrieking in their cages.
but shortly after,
he thrusts me upon the wall of the collar of my favorite blue
    turtleneck,
and screams that I'm nothing without him,
and so maybe its true,
so I cannot leave him,
I am far too afraid.

OCD

I tried to think of the hills by my house,
how I would roll down each blade of grass,
and comb through it with the tips of my fingers.

Thinking of my carefree five-year-old self spinning in big puddles of
    rain
letting it gather me up in a sopping lump.

The rain feels so dark now.
The sky opening its jaw wide and swallowing me whole,
the thought of feeling acidic drops running in snakes down my
    throat traps my breath in tight weaves.

When I was seven,
I felt safety being stripped from me
doing anything from standing in the middle of the hallway
to sitting on a bus stop bench.

This sudden breath being sucked from my lungs, my buttermilk skin,
growing sticky.

Simple tasks like brushing my hair or washing my hands took longer.
Time once like playing cards between my fingertips now morphing
    into water,
slipping between the cracks,
an entity I could not hold and put up against my skin.

I spent waking hours counting each tile on the floor,
thinking of oceans grabbing my mother by the hand and submerging
    her glass eyes,
because of me and my lack of checking in on her.

I couldn't touch countertops or pens,
the floor grabbing me by the hair and trying to pull me deeper.

I often cried,
hoping the tears wouldn't fall into my pores.
Obsessed with the things that hurt me,
and avoiding reflections that showed my deep black holes of eyes
and pale skin.

Like a promise
I often repeated to myself:
Please let me be safe.

ANGER

Nobody Believing
I Had an Eating Disorder

That day the sun and moon were quiet,
patiently waiting to see what I would do.
The cafeteria was loud,
food smeared on the tables, and juice spills on the floor.

I looked at my brown paper bag, and the jungle that surrounded me,

My friends laughed,
food spitting out of their mouths,
cookies, candy, and pizza spilling out of their bags,

Why aren't you eating?

I saw their mouths move,
but it didn't connect with what they meant.

Because days before the rain poured through the school yard,
wind shaking the basketball hoops
and they howled and laughed at what they called fat people.

I went to the counselor her bangs blunt
and sharp black hair cutting through her voice.

She left me with the words
you are never going to be anorexic; I have a friend who's anorexic
and you're not like her

One meal led into one day
soon it was months of just eating lies and torment.

I remember standing up in the same cafeteria a year later,
my vision growing weary,
my head hitting the concrete
they offered me raspberry tea,

[. . .]

the school nurse with curly brown hair
and my school counselor
What happened?

I felt her bangs still sharpening my cheekbones
and I looked at her
Maybe if you would have listened…

Panic Attacks in the Hospital

The night must have been quieter back at home,
the TV was probably droning on
while my mom held the blanket to her chest,
her sad face lit by the screen.

I imagined my cats sleeping peacefully,
dreaming of my brother's hands stroking each ear.

But in the hospital I could only hear my heartbeat
racing over the nurse's voices.
It was like the moon was a different one than the one my mom said
   goodnight to.

I felt my chest convulse,
and my throat close each side in
to kiss each other one time before departure.

I screamed on the blue mat,
the nurses surrounding me like thunder clouds.
Collecting their words like raindrops that rolled off my coat.

My hearing was dull,
I could only pick out a few words,
mostly the repeated ones:
breathe
safe
okay.
All of them made me angry,

Denver Children's Hospital

They gave me headphones with no wires.
And I walked to the window outside the emergency room
and watched the sun set its wings down below the oak tree.

I remember feeling jealous of the girls who sat in gray Hondas that
    rushed by,
they didn't have the heavy feeling that weighs down their chest,
or the indents in their arms from locked strips on a stretcher.

Earlier they asked me if I could go onto the stretcher myself.
I remember saying
I thought I was good at hiding it.
The nurse looked into my eyes and said,

*Honey, you don't have to have a bullet hole on your forehead
for us to be able to tell that you need help.*

And I screamed,
running barefoot down the hall while they trampled onto me,
pulling my arms behind my shoulders and strapping them to the blue
    stretcher.

It had been five months since I was allowed to go outside.
The air was so damp and dense that I felt like I could stick my spoon
    into it and shove it down my throat.
A lot of questions were asked,

Do you want anything to eat?

Do you know where you are?

How old are you?

Do you commit to staying alive if we send you back?

their questions felt like threats,
hanging my future above my head,
when will it be my turn to make my own choices?

I drew with yellow crayons on pieces of paper,
and cried to songs that bombarded my ears through the wireless
    headphones.

When they released me,
we walked through the intensive care unit,
flashes of bloody orange stretchers, neck braces, and breathing tubes.

They expected me to be happy,
like I was given bright gold balloons,
but even the next morning when I woke up in a brown loveseat
I clutched to my chest and could feel the emergency room bed
    leaning up against my spine.

It's not like it ever had an ending,
but just stuck like syrup on my palms.

To My First Boyfriend

I was just a child,
surviving on lies that you spoon-fed me.
I often wonder if you remember the day we met.
I do.

I was wearing a pumpkin-orange shirt that stared back at me in the
    mirror, with a mocking tone of *nobody will ever love you.*

And when I was heartbroken,
left with a laundry bin filled to the top with my sorrows
you decided I was your project you were going to fix.

I stood,
crying with your blue glacier eyes staring back at me,
and your brown hair breathing back and forth with the floor fan,
it's not your fault I never got a chance to search for who I am
but instead tried to figure out you.

I now know I could never figure out who you were
even if I knew you for twenty years.

By the time we were fourteen
I never saw your eyes any other colors but red.
I watched you sit
knees touching to other girls with pink lemonade lips
they would twirl your hair,
and you loved it,
looking at me with your side glance and frown.

Saying *love* felt like a promise I couldn't keep.
It felt easy for you,
but I had already given up so much of myself I couldn't lie as well.

I left you with the word
Taker
On your forehead.

MIRRORS AT DIFFERENT TIMES IN MY LIFE

1. ON THE DEATHBED OF ANOREXIA

The table lay lopsided behind me,
imagining my slanted room,
where my plants rolled onto the floor.

Crashing and burning like the decay I view in front of me.
I watered the plants tentatively
while slowly killing myself.

The white hanging box of a mirror stood, stuck in front of me.
The only light peering through was bright but bone-chilling.

I woke up screaming,
so right now at 11am I stood silently
trying to let the leftover noise drain out.

I stared with fury at my own eyes,
counting each vertebrae,
peeling apart my hollow cheeks,
and running my fingers over deep purple bags sagging down my skin.

I felt still,
but in the way that things move slower, not calmer.

[. . .]

2. Out of Elevators in the Waiting Room

My head hung low,
I grasped my arms
running over each tiny bump and groove with my fingers.
Even the hairs on my neck stood shaking with fear.

I stood in constricting big metal boxes,
dings reminding me to leave,
where I can breathe again,
the door widened its mouth,
and I rushed out.

I said sorry as I bumped into my own reflection.
Stepping back
the girl standing in front of me hollow,
empty.
Not even remembering looking in a mirror
before he took over the losing battle.

I quickly stepped out of the small room,
catching my breath.
For the first time I feel like I actually saw myself.

DEPRESSION

VIRTUAL VISITS IN TREATMENT

The room was quiet,
the other patients with their knees to their chests,
talking to computer screens.

My mom always tried to stay strong for me,
looking at my scrawny face,
and the tube hanging out of my nose.

She showed me my empty room
the coughing fireplace
the old carpet
and tried to force a smile
one where her cheeks puffed up, and her teeth hid behind her lips.

But she looked at me and said
I wait day and night in your empty bed, sometimes sleeping but mostly
  crying and feeling the sheets hold my hand when you're not there to
  grasp it. I miss you terribly, please work for me.

My heart aches,
I want to give her hope,
a phone call from my therapist
telling her I took a bite
I can just imagine her smile and tears that spring from her eyes.

but when the meal starts
the black bowl of strawberries hiss and glower at me,
my stomach pushes against the waistband of my pants
and I find myself with my face buried in my knees.
I let her down every day.

To My Childhood Best Friend

It's six in the morning and I can't remember your voice.
The soft purr,
or loud belly laugh
that swung back and forth over the rope swing we used to go on.

I wonder what you look like now,
I still remember the pale-yellow house
that stood out among the vines,
or how we'd sit on the hanging bench,
wisteria floating above our heads.

We used to rake up the leaves and bury our faces among the pile,
Singing together in carpeted garages
that echoed our voices.
Or when I told you I felt alone
and you held onto my hand in the light August sun,
while I brushed past the word:
Anorexia.

You told your mom,
and she stuck it into the drawer filled with,
thumbtacks, old papers, envelopes ,tissues,
and hid it there.

You even asked if you could see me,
my last night at home,
but I raised my bony arms to reply,
I can't.

In my twin sized bed in treatment
I would watch the curtains hanging from the door frame
blow back and forth with each step the nurses took
and listen to my MP3 player
blaring *Two Door Cinema Club* in drugstore earbuds
and think of you
and our summer nights of sleeping on the trampoline
and talking till our voices grew hoarse.

It aches me that it is now 7 in the morning,
and I still can't remember your voice.

The Reality behind Instagram Posts

1. Cama Beach

The sunsets didn't paint my soul like they used to.
The orange stroking into the blue used to make me feel like I was
    floating
but when I stare
I still feel myself sink into the earth.

I sat in the thick of the forest
listening to the music of the trees swaying and the leaves rustling.

My mom paced through the woods on the telephone
speaking to a possible new therapist.

I was diagnosed three days ago
anorexia was carved into my skin.
She tried to bring foods I used to like
baguettes and cheese
I nibbled
tears seasoning each bite.

I could tell she thought this getaway would save me,
but I've already wilted.

2. Christmas Eve

I am supposed to be happy.
Feel the warmth of hot chocolate run down my throat,
bake cookies for Santa
and sneak one for myself hoping he wouldn't see

but I've been sitting at a table for 3 hours
and have finished half my sweet potatoes and chicken.

My young cousins keep asking me why I don't eat,
and why I cry at every meal.
Their beady eyes staring at me
and small faces forming a frown,
I would lie
it's all I'm good at these days
but I still feel the truth leak out my pores.

Even my hair comes out in clumps
when I comb my hands through it.

I barely recognize myself in the mirror anymore
the way that even the name *Genevieve*
doesn't have anything to attach to.

[. . .]

3. LOLO AND LOLA'S

My grandparents' house always smells like freshly made pandasal
and boiling sinigang.
The smell used to create a rush through my whole body,
but now even the scent of food turns up my nose hairs.

My Lola grabbed my arm,
you've gotten so skinny
Fear laced through her voice.
This comment would usually make me feel like I accomplished
    something,
the title of *skinny* on a gold medal.

But my heart bled when the words left her tongue

The Philippines is so enriched with food
a stuffed belly made people cheer
and you are never completely full
according to my aunties and uncles.

When my parents told them I wasn't eating,
I stood at the top of the stairs
listening to the shock in their voice
because I used to devour every meal they gave me
but my eyes landed on the scale in the dim lit bathroom.
And every voice from downstairs was muffled,
the only clarity I got was my weight.

To My Friend I Met in Treatment

Do you remember the day I met you?
How your black hair was so fine it rubbed against your cheek
like straw,
and when I sat down next to you,
your blue coat rubbed against mine,
while tears rans down your pale cheeks,
chasing after each other as you begged for your mom.

We used to sit and watch the storm brew from three stories high.
We would wonder silently if the black suspended skies were like a
    shirt God could wring out.

Both desiring freedom,
to feel the wind cascade over our skin,
and that the thick of the hospital would have an opening
so we wouldn't be listening to each other's screaming
but the beating of the earth's heart.

Your mom would visit you often.
Most visits were quiet,
squeezing hands, kissing cheeks, embracing, braiding hair.

Your voice,
so soft
not even your mom could hear the low murmur of your words.

She would play you music,
hoping to pick you out of the roll call of names,
and scoop your body in a way where you at last remember
what love feels like,

[. . .]

because the picture hanging on your wall had your young self
running with open arms
and a wide smile,
the camera,
your drop of liquid gold.

Your voice is still engraved in my skull
as if you carved your initials in the stump of my body.

Girls with glasses told me you are again gone,
the spice in their voice thick and sticky.
Painting out for me that you're in hospitals,
tears streaming down your cheeks

I try to remember your sweet face,
or how you'd hold my hand down the hall and whisper
you got this.
But I'm tired of crying and wishing you were here with me now.
It's like knocking on a tree and expecting it to answer.

IN THE VOICE OF MY BROTHER

My house is no longer a home,
every room has a stale stench of sorrow.
Meringues of snow droop on my hood every time I leave.
The quiet hum of city lights is now my only escape from your
    screams.

I often trace' my fingers over the tables spine when I arrive home.
Your voice is still chasing me and falling onto my dinner plate.
I can still smell your blood and the pools that you left me with in the
    bathroom.

While my mind freezes over,
and my lips turn blue,
our parents cradle you.

I never demand attention,
getting the role of the tree while you leapt across the stage.
but your vacuum teeth have sucked every ounce of support from
    Mom and Dad,
no matter how much I cry their eyes stay glued to you.

You try to call me, but your voice always breaks into tears,
talking about the four years of hell and I don't find the words like I
    used to,
they lie in my alphabet soup and melt slowly with boiling water.
I wondered at the beginning if this was my fault,
if I lit the wick on the candle,
when I could've just cut it off.

But resentment infected my brain.
The nasty things you say that leave blood trailing down our parent's
    cheeks fill me to the brim with rage.

I miss you though, I truly do, but I do not miss your disorder.

SILENCE IS LOUDER THAN SHRIEKS

I tried to remember home.
The thick cracked cassette tape of noise humming softly,
while my hand strummed the wheel.

Or the busy night on the streets,
where I'd hear people's keys jingling and alarming cars.

In the hospital room,
things were quiet.
I couldn't hear the cars outside,
I'd see them roam like cows over the pasture,
but I couldn't hear their low hum as they came closer to the entrance.

The snow that fell had no noise,
even when I'd see people walk out with blankets wrapped around
    their bodies,
I couldn't hear the crunch of their footsteps
or the slurp of hot chocolate.

Things felt duller,
When I called my mom she described the empty streets
with people who'd swerve at the sight of her
the world so covered with fear that a cough could cause a car crash.
I felt like breathing was wrong in the noiseless world.
My arm often hung out of our leather loveseat like it was numb,
the only sound, my stomach grumbling in sporadic episodes.

I'd watch my breath go in and out,
while his voice grew louder and louder in my tongue.

EATING DISORDER

[trigger warning for purging and restriction]

My eyes were open before she touched the light switch.
I could hear her voice say *wake up*
but the black gravestones of bags under my eyes left me
sinking into the bed.

Food has no taste anymore.
I don't have to eat it to know that.
White swirls of plates that carry brown slabs of toast,
and the grapes, once my favorite fruit, stare at me like crying eyes.

Yesterday I tried to write.
I had blank sheets of paper glaring back at me for hours.
I wanted to describe the torture.
The way I crawl out of bed flinching at my shadow
because I know the stretched-out figure is a fake
that will trick me into happiness,
or how at 9 a.m. I coughed up blood
and still can't seem to quit purging my insides.

tears stained my skin,
as he looked into my blank stare,
you always play the victim,
you should know by now all I've done is help you
I was taught that my voice was a weapon against myself.

I stopped writing,
the only thing that brought true joy within me was taken away
because he told me I didn't deserve it.

It's been three weeks since I've seen my
parents. I miss my mom's sweet voice,
the way that she'd hold my hand
and rub the small of my back.

[. . .]

I tried calling her until morning, describing the pain.
How when I look at myself in the mirror
the most color in my skin is my yellow feeding tube.
How when I breathe it feels like I'm suffocating.

she paused,

This is all because of him.
you need to get rid of your eating disorder.

I remember feeling knots in my stomach,
staring at the black telephone in disbelief and hanging it up.

I cried all night,
it was so far from what I wanted.
The phone calls are the closest I'll be to her,
but she doesn't understand.

My therapist looked at me today,
pushing her glasses up the bridge of her nose.
Why do you listen to him?

I thought of the days with him.
Where I sat, my knees to my chest,
his voice shattering mine.
Pain running through every inch of me,
and watching my thighs inflate like balloons,

because even though I know he can't physically kill me,
he will wrap and rot and torment me till I have no other choice.

So I shut my eyes tight,
exhaling,
replying with,
I need him.

FEBRUARY 10TH, 2020

IN MY BROTHER'S VOICE

When we were little, you used to hold your breath
around people with cigarettes between their lips.
I would laugh and take big inhales as if I was smoking myself
while you'd swat the leftover smoke away.

It was eleven that night and in one hand I held my beer
and in the other a cigarette that didn't have to hit my lungs
to know that I wanted it.

Something about your text felt small to me
like your voice was hiding behind the curtains
and the window was never opened to let the anxiety drip
out but held shut to help you spiral.

The blue text said:
can you come home? I need to tell you something.

Mom and dad spent a lot more time these days with you,
looking at your toilets before you flushed,
holding your hand as you leaned against them
tears on both your shirts,

And maybe that night I didn't want to admit it,
but I just looked at the message five times over
and thought of the house,
how your room left a red stream of light
pouring through the living room,
or how the door swung on its hinges and awoke you within seconds
because you never sleep anymore,
how Mom and Dad no longer kiss
but instead hold each other and cry.

And I texted you back,
can we talk tomorrow?

[. . .]

But the next day came, and I sat on the porch from 5 to 11
and realized
you weren't coming back.

INSOMNIA IN TREATMENT

[trigger warning for self-harm]

Quiet used to be so comforting,
with the only sound being snow hitting the grass,
and the curtains blowing back and forth.

But it's midnight and with the flashlights clicking off and on
to check on what's supposed to be my sleeping body,
and the sounds of badges hitting each proximity card reader
make it so that I can barely close my eyes.

Sometimes I would spoon feed myself memories,
trying to think of seven-year-old me dancing in the living room with
    my parents.
or how I used to make cardboard cakes for my dolls,
but it would always come back to the past three years.

How I started from diets and exercise to carrots and cucumbers
to nothing at all.
Even with being so full of memories it felt better than being full
of mashed potatoes and steak.

I would often check to make sure my roommate's eyes were closed
and that the door was almost shut but not all the way so the nurses
    wouldn't yell at me,
and I would watch my sheets cover with blood,
thinking that it would make me feel better
but most of the time I just felt worse.

I wanted to end my nights the way I used to end poems when I first
    started writing,
with a big realization and tied up nicely with no thoughts after,
but I stopped writing that way because it wasn't real.

No nights ended with a sigh and release from the memories
that etched themselves in my skin
I don't even remember ending most of them
just resting and waking up the next morning to the same thing.

TREATMENT CYCLE

I went to treatment for the first time when I was 13.
I remember how my family got up at six a.m.
not really waking from anything,
because none of us slept that night.

The road was quiet.
Like raindrops could hit and no sound would come out of each
    puddle.
It was at that point the sun couldn't wave to us
because its arm was lazily held behind each mountain slowly rising.

I often wished I could rise like the sun
slowly and steadily reaching with each arm
but I jolt when I wake,
my arms freeze,
and when I stand with a blanket cape,
my head almost always kisses the floor
from the blackness that covers my eyes.

When I arrived,
people typed aggressively
and stared at each person who rang the doorbell with a perfect smile,
the cameras stared me down
the doors closed heavily
the staff watched when I would stand for too long.

My head felt heavy on the pillow,
all I wanted to do was sleep but nothing in the world could make me,
I sat in my wheelchair and watched them force yellow tubes down
    my nose.

I was 13.
The age where most girls get their periods,
and get their first phone,
and have a birthday party where boys are invited.
I was 13.

But I watched winter turn to spring,
I watched the snow melt and thaw on each branch,
I watched my eyes lighten with the sun,
I watched the cherry blossoms start to flourish,
and I thought to myself *I am okay*.
But I was moving with the season, not recovery.

Growing Up

I often question when the time was
where I let my imagination bleed out of my skull
and my mouth fell like bleeding ink on a newspaper.

I didn't laugh at jokes anymore,
I didn't want to sit on the woodchips of my elementary school
and laugh at my friends hanging from monkey bars.
And the worst part was I didn't know if this was growing up
or if this was depression.

My dad's hair started to fall out when he was forty,
mine when I was 12.

My mom started to get gray hairs when she was forty-two,
and I didn't want to ask but I couldn't tell why my hair stayed brown
while my insides faded to gray,
but I asked her *did you grow gray in there too*
pointing at her chest,
and she dropped the pasta that we were looking at in the grocery
    store and said,
don't say things like that.
Like I had stung her with my thorns that no longer had a rose at the
    top.

Birthdays started to feel like funerals,
I didn't want to grow up.

I wondered why we lit pretty-colored candles
for a day that was taking me farther away from happiness
and closer to stress.

I started to become obsessed with the ten-year-old body,
I didn't want a curved chest and round butt,
I wanted to look young so I didn't have to feel the pain of growing.

But I became ten again,
or as close to it as I could,
and I ruined being a child too.

The Cold of Anorexia

My Lolo often liked to go for long drives.
I would stick my tongue out the side of my mouth
and let the summer wind cascade over my cheeks.

It was in December of 2017 that we packed ourselves in the car,
even with the red glow on the heater I could feel each bone stinging
    with cold.
Nothing could make me feel that tingly warm heat in my chest,
I could barely move without shivering.

I wore sweatshirts often,
The kind that hung below my knees and swung on my bony arms.
When I developed anorexia, I lost the light inside of me
which might explain how my body did the same,
no candle to warm me.

I would run home from school every day,
my body aching.
And when I arrived, I would sit my back against the heater.
The cold metal slats burst with warmth that I didn't have.

Often I wouldn't even bother to turn the lights on.
My mom would come in with a big red strainer of *I'm sorry*.

But I would ask her to leave out the dragon's mouth of my door,
    because I didn't want her to be swallowed like I was.

Suicide Note

Tears fumble down my skin,
my pain falling like snow,
building mounds atop garden beds, rattling my dry bones.

I stare out blank windows,
bare streets,
and lay with full notes on the foot of my bed.

My mother once told me
it's like I lay with a log in the middle of chilling oceans,
no boat to row,
just clutching onto it.

She depicted her hands stretched out,
ready for me to grab them,
my defiance held strong,
gasping and heaving in piles of liquid ice.

But now I write to her
It's not an act of defiance anymore,
but more weakness, hopelessness under him.
I don't know if I'll ever be free, so let me go.

Treatment in Colorado

I watched them leave,
glimmers of my mother's long ginger locks swishing on her back.

My dad,
stopping in his tracks,
goodbye Genevieve.

My heart sank,
weeping into white pillows
while the night carried me into the depths of terror.
The sun flaked through the mountains.

Dawn bringing heavy weighted rooms,
they pulled my arms behind my spine,
forcing yellow down my nose,
my screaming filling up the deflated room with one big exhale.

My legs held down,
as if I were an animal,
roaring from my stomach,
snarling my teeth,
but not even animals like to be kept in cages.

That week I sat beside fake fireplaces,
breathing heavily into my knees,
tears fluttered their little wings down my skin.

My knees to my chest,
nobody likes you,
he hushed,
so I lay my mouth sealed.
While girls collected in puddles,
whispering my name.

My mom's letters held tightly in my hand
I miss you.
The grimace that must strike her face,
but at least pain gets to see her,
I don't even remember what her voice sounds like.

Taking Up Space

In grade four I let noise bound out of me,
down grassy patches,
my hands touched below me,
cartwheels through dirt filled paths.

I let my voice carry down the block,
lifting up those silenced,
carrying them in the drifts of wind.

I sang,
my voice belting in gymnasiums,
black hats on my head,
purple feather boas around my neck.

Ridiculous they called after me.
The words stirred in the air.
Starting to wince at recordings,

and avoid dinner knives,
the reflections taunting me.

My seat filled
but desperately begging to be empty.

I tried to blend into the drywall,
bland landscapes.
Nobody could argue with the mute.

I hid behind thick blankets of darkness.
Pouring my soul into black journals
questioning whether to be heard or not.

I now let the noise carry me,
floating by swarms of children.

My somber face,
blending into school pictures,

hurt in my eyes.
Sometimes I venture back to grade four in my head and wonder
what would have happened if I didn't go silent.

"God Has a Plan"

The grandfather clock swung in the silence,
my insides churning
God watches all.

My Lola licked off the words,
her hand squeezing my knee.

I always pondered God
and where he stands while he gazes through blankets of black
where stars shine to nobody in particular

through Rocky Mountains,
falling hills,
streaks of green
with wet flakes of snow slapping his skin.

I wonder if he can see me
in the tops of sleepless buildings,
so delicate
rubbing my pale skin
eyes welling with tears.

Why would he set me up to fail time and time again?

I sat in a silent room,
my knees pressed against cement floors,
praying out:
please don't let me be God's mistake.

DEAR DEPRESSION

When I was eleven,
I picked up the debris of lost friendships
and sat alone at the top of a tree.
Loneliness in a way was safer than getting hurt again and again.

My life felt like the leaves I watched fall in front of me,
every memory being stepped on by school children,

and getting hidden under piles of wood chips.

You stood behind my back,
I felt your cold hand squeeze my shoulder,
and press decay into my pores.

Fewer and fewer people heard me speak,
Your voice was filling me up too much
that all I could get out were a few mumbles.

Your once softening tune grew more serious.
The days we would spend in bed,
my body pressed against yours
where I would listen to our hearts match pace,
now were spent with deviating plans on how to hurt myself.

They told me you were hurtful.
But while he grasps me by the hairs on my neck
and screams that I am nothing without him,
you hold my hand and twirl my hair
telling me that sleeping can make it stop.

ON THE WAY
TO DENVER EATING RECOVERY CENTER

My mom squeezed my hand the whole plane ride,
soft whispers of *I love you*,
the words digging me deeper under the blanket of blue light.

My eyes caught on the wind of seven p.m.,
I gazed behind me,
trying to rein the tears back in,

a wrinkled woman held herself under a quilted blanket
silent tears rolling down her cheeks,
meeting mine,
connected in the worry of never arriving home.
Denver was caked in snow when the plane came to a halt.
The hotel was quiet,
small,
but not nearly as empty as I felt.

I stirred my finger in the bathtub,
I used to love baths,
music swirling in the air,
bubbles up to my chin,
but this bath was silent.

My legs rattling in lukewarm water
I felt like I was crawling in skin that didn't belong to me.
all the rage and fear has sunk to the bottom of the tub,
and I'm left with desolation clinging to my bare limbs.

Room-Based Care

The bed was dressed every morning.
White stiff sheets that crunched when you rolled over in your sleep.
I began to find amusement in the changing color of the quilted
  blanket each day.

Sometimes green or purple or brown or yellow.
It was the only thing that changed for months.

I was told to sit on my stiff bed all day.
The weakness of my body that they described
knocked down the strength inside me as well.

I used to think silence was peaceful,
and that every word was delicately wrapped and given as a gift
when the silence ended.

I never thought that it would be all I heard.
The ringing in my ears,
the only sound being the beeps of machines
and crunching of sheets.

I barely spoke anymore.
My vocal cords were a void in my throat.
I tried to remember how my laugh sounded,
or how it was heard when I spoke loudly, and it wasn't screaming.

I felt dangerous,
my words now daggers ripping through the wrapping paper.

I never wanted to hurt anyone.

REDEMPTION

Genevieve as a Ghost
Watching Her Eating Disorder

The walls were cold against my limbs when I woke.
I have always been a night owl, but this exceeds that.
I watched you toss and turn,
till the sheets were on the floor.

And this morning my mom opened the door quietly,
afraid to wake you.
and sat at the edge of your bed,
soft sobs creeping in between each finger.

When you woke
your screams scared birds perched in the trees outside the house.
But when standing, my mom had to catch you,
so weak from screaming your eyes would roll back.

Your words were simple
No. no. no.
I can't. I can't. I can't.

I sat at the table with you,
while you kept forgetting that you already asked mom
why eat? there is no reason.
five times in the past 10 minutes,
so you kept repeating it while she answered
weaker and weaker each time,
to keep you out of the hospital

I know you can't hear me or see me anymore.
But I wish you could
because I miss having arms that I could hug my mom in,
and legs that I could walk in,
and a mouth that I could laugh in.

[. . .]

I don't know if you remember,
but we used to be happy,
the kind of happiness where your eyes were stars
and people would stare at the glimmer.

And I know you hate the word healthy,
because you think it means your stomach
hanging over the waistband of your pants,
but I also think you hate the word healthy
because you know this is unhealthy
and you don't want to lose this.

but you were healthy once,
your thick hair glistened like flakes of gold.
and pink roses bloomed in your cheeks,
your nails were strong and didn't fall off and break,
and you could go on runs with my mom without collapsing.

I wish you could see how beautiful that is.

To Dad

The clatter of pots and pans shakes the house when you cook,
you dance around the kitchen in your black apron
singing along to the *Tragically Hip* at full volume,
noise had no boundary when you were happy.

When my life was just beginning to sprout,
I viewed you as my hero
in a red cape and yellow tights.

I loved how our voices ran together in perfect harmony
and how the scroll of ideas was always endless.
We would even chuckle at the same parts of every movie.

Bright tabloid covers and blaring television had attached an
    unspoken rule to me.
That the light from my soul had to be crushed
and I was supposed to be there to kneel at the feet of others
because I am a woman.

I saw the casket of what I dreamed of
dying filled with the half of me you brought onto this earth.

I screamed my voice hoarse at you,
countless nights where you'd shout back
at my unnerving howl through wine-stained teeth,
because I wounded you time and time again,
but Dad, doesn't it make sense now? You were only but a vessel.

GRATITUDE

I live for winter nights,
the moon shines brightly on the tip of my nose
as I listen to the earth's cries hit the concrete with a soft pitter-patter
    of tears.
The trees breathe with me,
in and out I can watch the leaves softly sway.

I often think about my sadness fossilizing,
watching my tears squeeze themselves down the shower drain,
a release with the gusts of wind from my lungs,
I hope my tears find peace in between the layers of the earth
and give life to the plants that must squirm their way to the top.

I used to view the world as if it was colorless,
I didn't find joy in snowflakes slapping my skin,
or how the steam from my hot coffee would warm my face.
Even my cat's purr wouldn't soothe me to sleep.

I didn't realize how much I took my life for granted till it was gone.

A Letter to a Song

"For Scientist Studies" by Death Cab for Cutie

You pull the tide out from under me,
peeling back my cocoon of sorrow
and scooping me out of hiding.

The portal of your cries,
we fall into memories
to catch my younger self's tears before they drown her

While the moon waxes and wanes
we plant roses with the suffering that leaks out of me
and dance in the grass while they grow.

When everything morphed into new,
you stayed the same,
my constant

Happiness

I didn't feel true happiness until I was 16 years old.

At ten it was in pink frosted birthday cakes,
and playing dress-up in my purple-painted room.
I was happy,
but not the type of happiness that I fought for every day,
and not the type of happy that you feel in each bone,

In treatment, they would ask for everyone to write their values on a slip
   of white paper,
I refused to write happiness,
because I thought it was a myth.

I viewed my depression as inexorable.
I wanted to wait till the clouds parted so I could see the sun again.
I didn't realize that happiness is like composing a song.
I created it myself by writing each note.

On my last day in the Eating Recovery Center,
the green walls that were once so frightening became a calming olive.
And my doctor looked at me and said,

you built this, protect it with everything you have,
nobody can break what you created because you are strong,
and you know how to hold to something even when someone wants it to go

Going Home from Treatment in Denver

The air was still inside,
my mind washed over each giggle and loud voice;
all I could hear was my breath.

It had been seven months since I had seen my family.
I had forgotten the aroma of my mother's perfume,
the song of my brother's voice, and the light in my father's eyes.

I stood at the end of the hallway,
and tears found their way down my cheeks.
The moment that every scream, tear, meal, tube has led up to.

When I walked through the doors,
my mother was standing there,
glowing with her carrot hair, and a bouquet of flowers.

And for a moment I felt as if my lungs had no air left,
embraced in her arms,
she smelling like the ocean.

I missed you and I will never leave again I promise

March through the Years

March 2018

The tiles on my ceiling started looking like racetracks,
my eyes moving faster than any car.
But even as a driver I feel trapped.
Every road comes to an end no matter how far I go.

I can feel his palm in the small of my back
as I sit from eight a.m. to ten p.m.
on my brown comforter.

My therapist wants me to think harder,
her pen tapping on yellow notepads,

But all I can think about is the pole with two bags
filled with a creamy substance pumping into my stomach.
I can't hear anything else.
The rattling noise blocks out every other voice.

My mom's face is hollow,
her cheeks sink into her white skin,
as she tells me over and over to eat.

But the food stares at me with big black eyes
and tells me to keep my mouth sealed.
I don't know who to trust anymore.

March 2019

I feel different,
I can barely recognize myself in the bathrooms where my wheelchair
    doesn't quite reach the sink.

I think often about silver blades
and ways to kill everything inside of me.

Every therapy session my mind rattles like dice
always landing on two.
The first thought is of deserving nothing,
and the second is of deserving pain.

I can barely look my mom in the eyes.
The way she looks at me,
I can tell I've broken her.

The tiles on my ceiling now look like an escape plan.
Popping one through and crawling till I no longer smell the fear on
    me.

The only one I trust is him and his ash eyes and bony face,
everyone else has let me fail.

[. . .]

MARCH 2020

Pain has a new meaning in my body.
It rushes into my blood
and makes my breath get trapped in between each lung.

I have a hard time talking to my mom on the phone,
even though all I want is to hear her voice,
he grips his claws into my skull every time she says *don't listen to him.*

My mom is 1,315 miles away,
I haven't seen her in a month.

My pencil barely touches paper anymore,
he screams at me to not let them know the torture he puts me
  through.

I haven't eaten since February,
I sit with my knees to my face and cry six times a day.

I only think about death as a release,
so I can finally end my suffering.
I don't trust anybody anymore,
I can't hear anyone else but him.

March 2021

This is the farthest I've gone without the low hum of hospital lights,
and the stomp of therapist's boots.

I feel like I'm missing something.
Every day is so new,
bundled up in red Christmas wrapping,
I never know what I'm going to get.

It's not perfect,
I still feel tears run down my cheeks every week or so.
But I no longer listen to him,
my ceiling looks like stars and endless possibilities.

I trust myself more than anyone else.

SPRING HEART

I stared at the basket as I spoke,
flowers sprouting even with the winding down of night.

Tears ran down my cheeks as my mother spoke to me over the black
    telephone,
Speaking of the garden she was planting for me
pale pink peonies—big heads bobbed and pressed into my window,
and hydrangeas blooming deep lilac,
little flowers working to create such large spectacles of light.

She described the ocher light,
and I began to think of summer nights as a little girl,
spinning in yellow dresses that created big wide puddles of fabric
    when I fell to my knees,
the trees used to bow to me
waving their long arms
rustling my hair.

But I thought of night,
long walks in winter
the flowers drooping over sides of clay pots,
snow falling slowly
piling on my eyelashes as I rub my coat to my upper lip,
everything so still
so violently silent.

I could hear my thoughts speak
the room to breathe
but my breath still collapsed into my lungs,
twisting my fingers waiting for spring.

So as I hung up the phone,
I waited till the sun went down and let them speak to me
all the dark winter spirals of thought
and even with tears running down my skin
I realized the promise of spring and flowers will not help me

I needed to find the flowers deep in the bushes of me
and curl on the dew dropped petals
for nobody can save me but myself

Things I Was Once Afraid of

I used to be afraid of my belly becoming a pit that let food buy space
    to live there forever.

I wanted approval from the world,
whether that was a smile or a superficial compliment.

I wanted to look at models on posters in the mall as reflections.
I thought of food as the enemy screaming at me holding a gun to my
    head.

I was so scared of making my anorexia mad that I succumbed to him
    and laid at his feet in fear.

I repeated his words in my head not knowing I was getting
    brainwashed.

And after nine weeks
of no food
or water
just a tube rushing nutrition into my body
I took a bite.

The cucumber was cold
and moist.
I felt my body tense and my breath swirl in my lungs.

I now eat when my stomach sends a handwritten letter to my brain
  letting me know that I'm hungry.
Anorexia would say I'm out of control.
But I finally have control back.

I sit on my black cotton loveseat with the forever idea that the reality
  of my fears is not as scary as my imagination makes them.

I Deserve(d) Better

Our shirts intertwined and let loose repeatedly
my cream sweater and your band tee,
hanging loosely on the thin line of string,
one gasp of wind and it would all fall like paper, painfully slow.

I remember when we sat on the oak tree,
you were always one branch above me
and I felt the sap stick to me as I'd climb up.

I pulled out my lungs and told you to breathe for me
believing that to prove my trust to you,
the trust in myself had to wilt.

I left your name carved into my skin.
I thought I loved you.

But love isn't waiting in a leather chair,
three hours past when you'd say you'd come,
watching the sun crawl back behind the trees
and couples walking hand in hand down the sidewalk
wishing that was us.

Love isn't you making other girls giggle
and taking their breath and moving it into yours.

Love is taking your soul and showing it completely,
every moment of shame and hurt.
I feel like I didn't even know you.

You had a constant spout of lies pouring out your mouth,
and I wrote on March 2nd, 2020
that I didn't deserve any better,
but now I know I do.

DREAM

I used to pour my dreams on restaurant placemats with a blue and
    red crayon,
at five my thoughts were all fantasies.

And I dreamt of sitting in Paris, France,
in a cafe where there were red umbrellas above me
shielding the sun that couldn't stop shining
and eating croissants with chocolate in the middle.

I dreamt of singing in front of an audience with a big belt and roar of
    my voice.

And somewhere along my journey of life I stopped dreaming.
My words became the monotone voice of what others fed to me.

I wanted to be skinny just like the other girls I sat with at lunch.
But never once did I laugh.
I may have giggled but never once did I feel a belly laugh
one that made my face hurt from the smiling.

When I stopped dreaming, I became small.
I was never meant to be small.

I am meant to have the passion that fires within me when I'm in love,
I am meant to fight off the voices that tore me apart and put myself
    back together
with only a needle and a black spool of thread.
I am meant to sing as loud as I can into a microphone
with speakers blaring in front of an audience.

I am meant to dream of whatever I want to be.
Not be put into a basket of *realistic*
and not be fed what *I should do*, but do what I want.

TO MY 12-YEAR-OLD SELF

Some days the noise of me breathing is enough to wake you
your face stamped in red ink in my memory,
I can almost feel your cold hands
and see you look up at me even with empty arms.
Things changed so drastically about you
but I always noticed the same brown eyes
that once were looking up at mom
in a bundle of pink cotton blankets.

I wish I could sing to you
and try to pour light through your ears
to stop the gunshot bloodied sounds that rattle your mind.

I can still hear your cry
and sometimes when tears fall from my cheeks
they create a pathway for us to swim in,
for us to be connected.
And amidst the pools of tears,
I would show you the four-year-old you,
with a glowing smile,
and perfect little arms
and ask you, why hurt her?
she does not deserve to be starved.

I know it's hard to hear me amongst the shouting of your mind,
but I promise you the shipwreck will be homed by colorful fish
and the wildfires chasing you day and night will stop burning
and collapse into the sun,
ashes sticking to you at first but then allowing grass to sprout
and flowers curling around your laying body.

You thought for so long only others can save you,
but the only one who can truly save you is yourself,
and the scared bluebird you are
will rise from the nest as a bald eagle
soaring across the mountains you peaked
and oceans you've swam.

I never got to say it but,
I love you,
not because of the gap in your thighs or your slender shoulders,
but because you are a part of me,
and always will be.

PERSPECTIVE

Perhaps our torment is so hard to analyze because it's like watching rain
from inside a car window.

The droplets smother the glass,
but it's often hard to see the source.
For you need to roll down the window and listen to what the rain is
trying to say,
to see it fall.

Toxic Love

I searched for love in places that had a Do Not Enter sign on the
    entrance,
I believed that French kisses would fill the hole in my swollen heart
and that if someone else loved me,
their love was enough to fill the void of self-love.

I stayed with people that made me fight for their love
and left the ones that gave it to me every second.

My dying heart gravitated towards knives over spoons
and tears over boredom.

Love has never been an equation I've been able to solve.

I told my last lover
they always leave
and I was the one who walked out the door.

STORIES ARE MEANT TO BE HEARD

I don't remember at which point
the sun started to fall down into the palms of my hands,
and I felt an immense amount of pressure to rub it on everyone else

Or at which point
I boarded up the windows of my eyes to my mind and left it sealed
for nobody to hear.

I felt alone.
The long blue cotton blankets never reaching my toes,
and the sun and moon both making me sad no matter what purpose
they gave me.

I thought if I had fallen,
she would be free,
the girl in yellow dresses with thick hair and bangs
that the little me would be given away to the light,
and she would no longer be a goldfish in my mind pounding
against the glass.

But she would also never be heard again,
all her quiet whispers where syllables leapt out her tongue
would be silenced,
and she wouldn't be able to see tall trees turn into glass buildings
and say something about it.

I have a chance for her voice to be heard, and I desperately need
to take it.

I Choose

[trigger warning for purging and self-harm]

I waited for the day for the mirrors to stop yelling back at me,
waiting for my coating of stomach to stop looking unwanted
and feel needed.

I switched rooms in my house because the walls were still coated in
   blood splatter
even when pure white.

And I slept on the couch because I could still see the plastic bags
   filled with vomit
and the razor blades on my bed every time I looked at it.

I was afraid of the color yellow
because it reminded me of my yellow feeding tube that hung from
   my cheek.
The black puffer coat that hangs in my closet still has my sick body's
   touch
even four years later.

I'm not afraid anymore,
of the pots of pasta,
or the cups of frozen yogurt.

My body is my home,
the place that's felt every hug and cut and tear fall from its cheek,
It is the home that's been to the Philippines, Paris, Mexico, and
   Hawaii,
It has carried me even when I was weak.
It has held me even when I hated it.

I kept waiting to feel this way,
to feel the love pour from me.
But that's just it: All I was doing was waiting for the right moment
instead of realizing the moment is what I choose.

[. . .]

There is no beam that will glow on me,
no bittersweet song that will play,
no traumatic event that will make me change my mind,
because even after I felt hands grabbing my arms and pushing them
back,
even as I felt tubes pierce my nose for years on an endless loop,
it didn't make me change my mind.

Until I did—
Not anorexia
Not purge disorder Not OCD
Not depression Not anxiety Not PTSD Not ADHD
Me—
Genevieve Elizabeth Lardizabal.

EARLY PRAISE FOR
A STARVED HEART

Beautifully poignant, vulnerable, and real. Genevieve is an extraordinary writer who breathes life into every word. With vivid detail she brings you through her journey, the dark night of her soul, and into the light of her true self. A powerful must read.

—Nadia Ahrens, LICSW, Psychotherapist

A Starved Heart is a personal account of one person's journey back from the abyss that can be mental illness. From the multitude of diagnoses to the cycles of therapy and treatment that can feel fruitless, the messiness and breadth of difficulty of the journey is captured. At the same time, Genevieve shares who she is, and shows that at the core of it all, the person struggling is still human, with friends and family, needing love and company. *A Starved Heart* explores the transformations throughout her journey and leaves the reader feeling humility and gratitude towards this beautiful art we call life, the people living it with us, and the diverse challenges we will all encounter whilst living it.

—Calliopy Bluebell, a former patient

"And sometimes when tears fall from my cheeks, they create a pathway for us to swim in, for us to be connected." A visual artist of words, Genevieve Lardizabal's raw, honest, and powerful poems draw our attention and insist we not look away

—Veronica Baik

A Starved Heart is an impressive, provocative, passionate read that conveys considerable knowledge about the complexities of an eating

[....]

disorder, treatment, and recovery. Communicated through poetry, it is simultaneously a heartwrenching and heartwarming reading experience. I appreciated how Genevieve positioned the eating disorder throughout the text— as an abuser—as a male with whom she was embattled for her life. There is much to learn from her manuscript about family relationships and mental illness, gender, cultural and societal norms, as well as how professional 'help' is constructed and experienced by a young person's vantage.

—**Patti Ranahan, PhD, Associate Professor**
Graduate Program Director, Youth Work
Concordia University

ABOUT THE AUTHOR

Genevieve Lardizabal is a 18-year-old poet from Seattle, Washington. During her second stay in an eating disorder treatment center, she was put onto room-based care because of her resistance to recovery and her refusal to eat. Room-based care is where one must stay in their room from 8:00 a.m. to 10:00 p.m., and is only allowed out for meals, a one-hour therapy session and one hour of visiting with family. She was isolated and alone. No other patients were allowed to speak to her, and she wasn't allowed outside for five months. So many thoughts swirled in her head and without any output she felt trapped, so she began to write.

By the end of that year, she was published in Z Publishing House's *Washington's Best Emerging Young Poets of 2019* and spent the next three years writing her book *A Starved Heart*, which dives deep into her disorders and experiences that lead her to recovery after four years of treatment center and hospital stays. She dreams of becoming a therapist for eating disorders and running a narrative therapy group at a treatment center, teaching kids how to write through their pain, whether that's through poetry, storytelling, song writing, or journaling.

Instagram: @gene.vievepoetry

About The Poetry Box®

The Poetry Box, a boutique publishing company in Portland, Oregon, provides a platform for both established and emerging poets to share their words with the world through beautiful printed books and chapbooks.

Feel free to visit the online bookstore (thePoetryBox.com), where you'll find more titles including:

We're Not Real Anyways by maddie mitchell

Built to Last by Tara L. Carnes

What She Was Wearing by Shawn Avenigo-Sanders

The Screaming Silence by Lanser Howard

Tracking the Fox by Rosalie Sanara Petrouske

Elemental Things by Michael S. Glaser

Listening in the Dark by Suzy Harris

Signs by Emily Newberry

Soundings by David Gonzalez

This Is the Lightness by Rachel Barton

Earthwork by Kristin Berger

The Round Whisper of No Moon by Peter Kaufmann

My Husband's Eyebrows by Leanne Grabel

Sophia & Mister Walter Whitman by Penelope Scambly Schott

A Nest in the Heart by Vivienne Popperl

and more . . .